Energy Essentials

Renewable Energy

Nigel Saunders and Steven Chapman

Raintree

Chicago, Illinois

For information, address the publisher:
Raintree, 100 N. LaSalle, Suite 1200, Chicago, IL 60602

Printed and bound in China
08 07 06 05 04
10 9 8 7 6 5 4 3 2 1

Library of Congress Cataloging-in-Publication Data

Cataloging-in-publication data is available at the Library of Congress.

Acknowledgments

p.4/5, Science Photo Library/David Hay Jones; p.4, Science Photo Library; p.5, (top) Corbis, p.5, (mid) Science Photo Library/Sinclair Stammers, (bottom) Rex Features; p.6, Alamy Images; p.6, (bottom) Science Photo Library/ Kenneth W. Fink; p.7, Photodisc; p.8/9, Rex Features; p.8, Corbis; p.9, Getty Images; pp.10/11, Corbis; p.10, Getty Images; p.11, Science Photo Library; p.12, (top) Corbis; p.12 (bottom) Science Photo Library; p.13 Science Photo Library; p.14 (top) Corbis; p.14 (bottom) Photodisc; p.15, Science Photo Library/Alex Bartel; p.16, (top) Corbis; p.16, (bottom) Science Photo Library; p.17, Corbis; p.18 (top) Science Photo Library; p.18 (bottom) Corbis; p.19, Rex Features; p.20, Images/Imagebank; p.21 Photodisc (top, mid and bottom); pp.22/23, Science Photo Library/Alexis Rosenfeld; p.23, Alamy Images; pp.24/25 Getty Images/Imagebank; p.24 Oxford Scientific Films; p.25, Science photo Library/Burlington Electric Department/NREL/US, Department of Energy; pp.26/27, Ecoscene; p.26, Corbis; p.27, Science Photo Library/Prof. David Hall; p.28 (top) Corbis; p.28 (bottom) Rex Features; p.29, Action Plus; pp. 30/31, Photodisc; p.30 and 31, Science Photo Library; p.32 (top and bottom) Science Photo Library/Martin Bond; p.33, Science Photo Library/Martin Bond; p.34 (top and bottom) Corbis; p.35, Corbis/ Hubert Stadler; pp.36/37, Oxford Scientific Films; p.36, The Photolibrary Wales; p.37, Science Photo Library/Bernard Edmaier; p.38, Science Photo Library/Martin Bond; p.39, Rex Features; p.40 (right) Corbis; p.40 (left) Science Photo Library; p.41; Science Photo Library/Martin Bond; p.42, Science Photo Library/Colin Cuthbert; p.43, Science photo Library/Chris Knapton; pp.44/45, Science Photo Library.

Cover photograph of solar panels reproduced with permission of Robert Harding Picture Library

Every effort has been made to contact copyright holders of any material reproduced in this book. Any omissions will be rectified in subsequent printings if notice is given to the publishers.

Contents

Any words appearing in the text in bold, **like this,** are explained in the glossary. You can also look out for them in the "word bank" at the bottom of each page.

What Is Energy?

Energy is all around us. We can see light energy from the Sun, electric lamps, televisions, and computer screens. But there are lots of other types of energy that we cannot see. Invisible heat energy keeps us warm and cooks our food. The chemical energy stored in food helps us to move and grow. Energy is needed to make cars and airplanes move and to make music. Without energy, the world would be dark and cold. Nothing would move, and everywhere would be silent.

The joule is named after the British scientist James Joule (1818–1889). ∧

Energy and the joule

The unit we use to measure energy is the joule, J. You need 10 joules of energy to lift a 2.2 lb (1 kg) bag of sugar from the kitchen floor to a worktop 3.3 ft (1 m) high. This is enough energy to run a typical electric lightbulb for one tenth of a second.

Hydroelectric power stations use the energy in moving water to make electricity. ➤

Word store energy   ability to do work; light, heat, and electricity are types of energy
fossil fuel   fuel formed from the remains of ancient plants and animals

Energy resources

There are lots of different ways to get the energy we need for our everyday lives. Anything that stores energy or gives us energy is called an **energy resource**. Coal, oil, and natural gas are the most common energy resources. They are called **fossil fuels.** They are used in power stations to make most of the electricity we need, but they have some big disadvantages.

Fossil fuels **pollute** the **atmosphere** when they are burned, and they take millions of years to form. Once they have been used up, fossil fuels will be gone forever, so they are called **nonrenewable** energy resources. **Renewable** energy resources, such as hydroelectric power, are different. Since they usually do not pollute the atmosphere and they will not run out, they are very important.

FAST FACTS
Every day, the Sun bathes Earth with more energy than is stored in all the crude oil that has ever existed.

Find out later . . .

How can we cook food for free using the Sun?

Where does the energy needed by living things come from?

How can we get energy from the Moon without going there?

pollute   to add harmful substances to the air, water, or land
renewable   will not run out and can be replaced

5

Renewable Energy Resources

To understand what **renewable energy resources** are, it is helpful to know about **nonrenewable** energy resources. Coal, crude oil, and natural gas are the main nonrenewable energy resources. They are called **fossil fuels** because they formed from the remains of living things that died millions of years ago. They contain a lot of carbon, which releases a lot of **energy** when it burns.

From trees to coal

About 300 million years ago, huge swampy forests covered a lot of Earth. When trees in these forests died, the swampy conditions stopped them from rotting away. Thick layers of dead plants formed, one on top of the other. Over time, these layers were buried and crushed by mud and sand. **Chemical reactions** slowly warmed the crushed plants and **turned them into coal.**

Anthracite, a very hard, shiny type of coal, is over 90 percent carbon. It is found over 3 miles (5 kilometers) underground. $\wedge$

The Carboniferous period began around 360 million years ago and lasted 70 million years. When plants such as these died, they formed the coal that is mined around the world today. $\vee$

Going, going . . .

Coal is used to make a third of the world's electricity. This uses up two-thirds of the coal mined every year. There may only be enough coal to last another 300 years. Once it has gone, it will be gone forever.

6   ***Word store***   chemical reaction   change in which new substances are made and energy is given out or taken in

From tiny creatures to big oil fields

Crude oil and natural gas were formed from the bodies of sea creatures that died over a hundred million years ago. When the creatures died, they sank to the seabed and were slowly covered by layers of mud and sand. As they were buried deeper and deeper, the bodies were crushed by the weight above them. Chemical reactions heated up the remains and slowly turned them into crude oil and natural gas. The mud and sand eventually turned into rock, trapping the oil and gas underground.

Oil companies drill through the rock to reach the trapped crude oil and gas. Crude oil must be **refined** to separate the useful fuels from the other chemicals it contains.

. . . almost gone?

Half of the world's oil taken from the ground each year is used to run airplanes, cars, and other vehicles. Most of the rest is burned to heat buildings and to make electricity. At the rate the world is using oil, there may only be enough to last another 40 years.

Oil rigs like this one in the North Sea pump crude oil from oil fields buried deep under layers of rock. ➢

energy resource   source or store of energy, such as hydroelectric power or coal
refined   purified at an oil refinery

Toward an energy crisis

Earth's **fossil fuels** will run out one day, but it is difficult to know exactly when. Why is this?

Rare things cost a lot

Imagine that you are dying of thirst in a desert. How much would you pay for a glass of water? Probably a lot if it meant you could survive another day. It is a similar thing with fossil fuels. As supplies begin to run out, prices will rise as people scramble for the remaining tons of coal, **barrels** of oil, or cubic feet of gas. This means that coal mines and oil fields that are too expensive to use at the moment will become worth opening up. However, these, too, will finally run out.

This is part of the Trans-Alaska Oil Pipeline. ∧

There was a shortage of crude oil in the 1970s. This meant that there was not enough gasoline to go around, so it was **rationed**. These people are lining up to collect a small can of gas. ∨

Oil in the wilderness

Alaska is a state in the **Arctic**. Almost 200,000 barrels of crude oil are taken from here each day, which is enough to supply the United States with almost one fifth of its oil. The Trans-Alaska Oil Pipeline carries the oil 745 miles (1,200 kilometers) south to the port of Valdez.

FAST FACTS

The population of the United States uses its entire weight in crude oil every week.

Word store   Arctic   far north, where it is usually very cold
barrel   unit used to measure the volume of crude oil; one barrel is 42 gal (159 l)

Making it last

Imagine that you are in a desert again. This time you have a bottle of water. If you drink it slowly, the water will last longer. Fossil fuels will also last longer if we use them more slowly. Most modern cars are designed to use less fuel on their journeys than older models. New power stations are more efficient, so they use less fuel to make the same amount of electricity. Anything that wastes electricity also wastes fuel, so you can even help save fuel by switching off lights when you leave a room. But the fossil fuels will still run out, and before they do, they will have caused a big problem—**pollution.**

Saving light

Ordinary lightbulbs make both light and heat energy. The light is useful, but the heat is just lost to the surroundings, wasting electricity. Modern energy-saving bulbs make much less heat. They use less electricity to make the same amount of light, so they also save fuel.

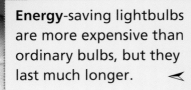

Energy-saving lightbulbs are more expensive than ordinary bulbs, but they last much longer. ◄

pollution harmful substances in the air, water, or on land
rationed given a fixed amount of something

9

Dying forests

Acid rain dissolves **minerals** in the soil and washes them away before trees can use them. This means that trees in areas where acid rain falls do not grow very well. They lose leaves and have less protection against **pests** and diseases.

These trees in the Czech Republic have been killed by acid rain. V

Pollution and the greenhouse effect

Coal is mostly carbon. When it is burned, it forms carbon dioxide gas. Oil and natural gas make carbon dioxide and **water vapor** when they are burned. The **fossil fuels** also contain small amounts of sulfur, which forms a harmful gas called sulfur dioxide when the fuels are burned. All these gases **pollute** Earth's **atmosphere** and harm our environment.

Acid rain

The sulfur dioxide made when fossil fuels are burned in power stations escapes into the atmosphere. At ground level, it can cause breathing problems. As it travels higher, it mixes with water vapor in the clouds to form **dilute** sulfuric acid. This falls to the ground with rain or snow. The acid damages buildings and kills living things in rivers and lakes.

This street in Mexico City is jammed with traffic during the morning rush hour. Waste gases are made when gasoline and diesel fuels burn in the vehicles' engines. They cause a thick, harmful smog. ʌ

dilute   mixed with another substance, usually water
mineral   substance needed by plants and animals to keep them healthy

The greenhouse effect

When the Sun's **energy** has passed through Earth's atmosphere, some of it escapes back into space as heat energy. Certain gases in the atmosphere are good at trapping this energy, so they stop some of it from escaping and keep Earth warm enough for living things. This is called the **greenhouse effect.** Without the greenhouse effect, Earth would be almost as cold as the Moon, which has an average surface temperature of 0 °F (–18 °C).

Carbon dioxide is very good at trapping heat in the atmosphere. Burning fossil fuels has increased the amount of carbon dioxide in the atmosphere, trapping more heat and increasing the greenhouse effect. This means that Earth is becoming warmer than it should be—a process called **global warming.** As Earth warms up, weather patterns will change and crops may no longer grow in some areas. The **polar ice caps** will melt, raising sea levels and flooding land near the sea.

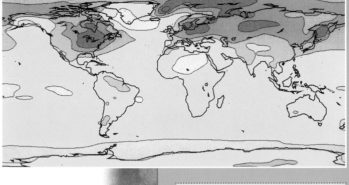

This map shows how much hotter the winters in the north would be if the amount of carbon dioxide in the atmosphere doubled. The red areas are 46–54 °F (8–12 °C) hotter than now.

Getting warmer

The amount of carbon dioxide in the atmosphere has increased from 0.0275 percent 300 years ago to 0.0365 percent today. This tiny change has been enough to increase average temperatures on Earth's surface by over 33 °F (1 °C)—and Earth is still getting warmer.

polar ice caps   ice covering the North and South poles of Earth

This traditional windmill in the Netherlands was used for pumping water. ∧

Renewable energy resources to the rescue

As we have seen, **fossil fuels** will run out one day and, in the meantime, they are **polluting** the **atmosphere** and causing **global warming**. An alternative to these **nonrenewable energy resources** is urgently needed. Luckily, there are several **renewable** energy resources that can be used instead. They will never run out, and they cause little or no pollution when they are used.

Five renewable resources

There are five main renewable energy resources, based on different types of **energy**. These are:

- light from the Sun;
- heat from the Sun;
- chemical energy stored in living things;
- the energy in moving air;
- and the energy in moving water.

Windmills

Windmills use **kinetic energy** from the wind to move machinery. The first windmills used this energy to drive machinery directly. The motion was used to pump water or grind wheat into flour.

The **solar** furnace in France uses 9,500 mirrors to concentrate the Sun's heat onto a furnace in the tower on the right. The furnace can reach a temperature of 6,900 °F (3,800 °C) and makes a **megawatt** of heat energy. ➢

generator   equipment used to make electricity
kinetic energy   energy of moving things

Renewable energy resources

Benefits

- Renewable energy resources are available all over the world.
- They will never run out.
- Once the equipment needed to use these resources has been built, it makes little **pollution** and **running costs** are low.
- Using renewable energy resources saves crude oil, which can then be used to make plastics and many other useful products.

Problems

- It can be very expensive to build some of the equipment needed. For example, The Aswan High **Dam** in Egypt, which is used to make electricity, cost one billion dollars.
- Renewable energy resources are not always reliable – you will only get electricity from a **wind farm** on a windy day and you cannot get energy from the Sun at night.

Windmills everywhere

Modern windmills usually turn electricity **generators,** changing the kinetic energy in the wind into electrical energy. They are often built close together in windy areas to make wind farms. These are noisy and can spoil the view in the countryside.

This wind farm in California provides enough electricity to power 100,000 homes. ⋀

running cost   cost of keeping equipment working
solar   anything to do with the Sun

Energy from the Sun

Without the Sun, the world would be a very different place. The temperature on the surface of Earth would be -454 °F (−270 °C), so cold that the gases from the **atmosphere** would be frozen solid. It would also be completely dark, with only the light from faraway stars to break the blackness. On a planet like this, there would be no living things at all, not even the smallest plant or animal.

Hot and bright

The Sun constantly bathes our planet with huge amounts of heat and light **energy** that we can use. When the Sun is shining, every square foot of Earth's surface gets enough **solar** energy to run over 100 electric lightbulbs at once. But **how can we trap this energy and use it in different ways?**

Drax in the north of England is Europe's largest coal-fired power station. ∧

Fire in the sky

The Sun is a huge ball of hot gases. The temperature inside it is so hot that hydrogen gas turns into helium gas. This releases huge amounts of energy— a hundred thousand **billion** times more than the largest coal-fired power station in Europe.

This is the Sun, the nearest star to Earth. The hot gases in the Sun move around, making swirling patterns on the surface. ➤

Word store   absorb   to take in
architect   designer of buildings

Cozy and warm

Buildings often become very hot on a sunny day. This is because a lot of the Sun's energy passes through the glass in the windows. The glass stops some of the heat from escaping and warms the rooms. The Sun's energy warms the walls and roof, too. This is called **passive** solar heating.

Trapping more energy

A building is in the best position to trap the most solar energy if it is built to face the Sun at midday—the hottest part of the day. Even more heat energy can be trapped if the walls are painted black. This is because **dull** black surfaces are very good at **absorbing** heat energy. Large windows will **trap even more heat energy—and all this energy is free.**

Too hot to handle

In very hot parts of the world, passive solar heating by the Sun is a big problem for **architects**. One solution is to paint the walls white to reflect heat energy. Large roofs are built to shade the walls. Shiny blinds can help keep a house cool on very sunny days.

This power station has been designed to make the most of passive solar heating. ⌄

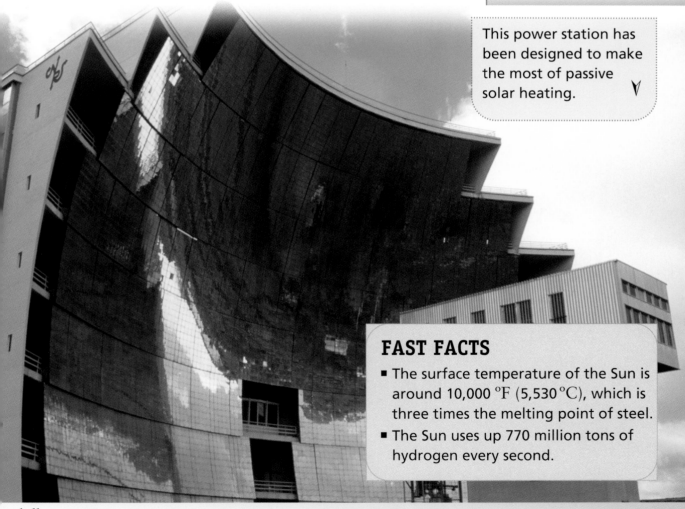

FAST FACTS
- The surface temperature of the Sun is around 10,000 °F (5,530 °C), which is three times the melting point of steel.
- The Sun uses up 770 million tons of hydrogen every second.

dull   not shiny
passive   something that happens with no machinery or extra energy needed

Cooking for free

Solar ovens use heat from the Sun to cook food. Shiny panels reflect the Sun's rays into the oven, which traps the heat and cooks the food. These ovens are very useful in sunny places far away from supplies of gas or electricity.

Solar ovens are used to cook food in Kenya. ⋁

Hot water from the Sun

Water for baths and showers is usually heated by a boiler that gets its **energy** from **fossil fuels** or electricity. **Solar** water heating systems use heat energy from the Sun to do the same job.

A thin, flat box called a solar collector is fitted onto the roof of a house so that it faces the Sun at midday. There are three layers in the solar collector. The outer layer is **transparent,** letting the Sun's rays pass into the collector, and the bottom layer is painted black to **absorb** as much heat as possible. Pipes filled with water run between these two layers. The water is warmed by heat energy from the Sun and stored in an **insulated** tank, ready for use.

This a solar water heating system on the roof of a house in Australia. The panels heat water for baths and showers. ⋁

focus   to concentrate into one spot
insulated   covered in material that reduces heat loss

Electricity from the Sun's heat energy

Electricity is made when an electrical **generator** turns. Normally, the **kinetic energy** in steam is used to turn the generator. The steam comes from water that has been boiled using the heat from burning fossil fuels.

Heat energy from the Sun can be used in a similar way. Solar tower systems use a large number of mirrors to **focus** the Sun's rays onto a tower. Often, the mirrors can move, and they track the Sun as the day goes by. The heat energy focused on the tower is used to boil water, making steam that turns a generator.

Solar dish systems use a mirror shaped like a large **satellite** dish to focus the Sun's heat energy. This heats a special liquid that **expands** as it gets hotter. The liquid pushes a **piston,** which turns a generator.

Sun traps

Trough systems use long mirrors with a special curved shape, called a **parabola,** to focus the Sun's heat energy on pipes running down the middle of the troughs. Oil flowing through the pipes becomes hot enough to boil water and make steam, which drives a generator.

FAST FACTS
Water boils at 212 °F (100 °C) and freezes at 32 °F (0 °C).

A technician checks the mirrors at a solar power station in the Mohave Desert in the western United States.◄

piston   moving cylinder in an engine or other piece of machinery
transparent   see through

Using the Sun's light energy

Solar cells change light **energy** directly into electricity without needing any liquids or moving parts. You may have seen small, square solar cells powering calculators that do not need batteries. Larger solar cells fitted into panels can **absorb** enough light energy to run much bigger devices.

Lots of light

Solar cells are very useful in areas with no electricity supply. It would be impossible to run an electricity cable up into space, so **satellites** have very large panels of solar cells to make the electricity they need. Back down on Earth, traffic signs and telephone booths far from the main supply get their electricity from solar cells. You can even buy garden fountains powered by sunlight. On a sunny day, solar cells on the roof may provide enough electricity for a whole house.

This is a single solar cell of the kind used in panels. ʌ

Chips with everything

Solar cells are made from the same types of materials used to make computer chips. When these materials absorb light energy, tiny electrically charged particles called **electrons** move through them. This is a flow of electricity. Converting light energy into electrical energy using solar cells is called the **photovoltaic effect**.

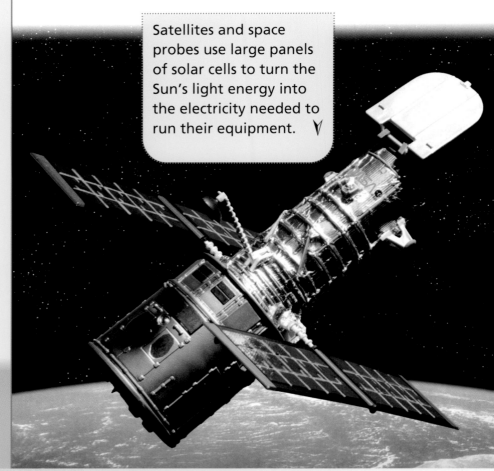

Satellites and space probes use large panels of solar cells to turn the Sun's light energy into the electricity needed to run their equipment. ⱱ

electron   tiny, negatively charged particle outside the nucleus of an atom
photovoltaic effect   converting light energy into electrical energy

Solar energy

Benefits

- Using heat and light energy from the Sun does not cause any **pollution.**
- Solar energy is a **renewable** resource, so it will never run out.
- **Fossil fuels** are conserved.
- The Sun's energy is free and it can be used wherever the Sun is shining, from your back garden right up into space.

Problems

- You cannot use the Sun's energy at night and there is less of it on cloudy days.
- Expensive batteries are needed to store electricity made during the day so it can be released at night.
- Some of the larger pieces of equipment that use the Sun's energy cost a lot to build. Solar cells are also expensive and often change just 15 percent of the light energy shining on them into electricity.

A car for the future?

There over 530 million cars powered by fossil fuels, and they create a lot of pollution. Solar cells could supply some of the energy needed by cars in the future. This would reduce the amount of gasoline or diesel used on each journey.

Some cars are already powered by solar cells.

Biomass Energy

A day in the life of Earth

Earth is about 4.6 billion years old. Imagine that this time is condensed into just a day. The first plants appeared 14 hours ago. Dinosaurs appeared, ruled, and became extinct an hour ago. And humans appeared just one second ago!

FAST FACTS

Photosynthesis by the world's forests uses about 99.2 **billion** tons of carbon dioxide every year.

Green plants grow toward the light so that their leaves can trap more energy. ➤

Using **solar** cells to turn light **energy** from the Sun into electrical energy is a new idea. But plants have been trapping and using the energy in sunlight for around three **billion** years.

From light energy to chemical energy

Green plants use a process called **photosynthesis** to turn light energy into chemical energy, which is stored as glucose and other sugars. Because they can make their own food, plants do not need to eat. Photosynthesis uses water from the soil, carbon dioxide from the air, and light energy from the Sun.

carbon dioxide + water + light energy → sugars + oxygen

Most plant **cells** contain a green substance called **chlorophyll** that traps light energy. Many plants have wide **leaves to trap as much sunlight as possible.**

Word store   cell   tiny building block of living things
cholorophyll   green substance that absorbs light energy, found in plants

Food chains and food webs

Animals cannot make their own food. They must eat plants or other animals to get the energy they need to grow and move. For example, rabbits eat grass and foxes eat rabbits. The grass gets its energy from sunlight, the rabbits get their energy from the grass, and the foxes get their energy from the rabbits. This relationship between plants and animals is called a **food chain.**

The arrows point from the living thing being eaten toward the animal doing the eating. Every food chain starts with a plant, because they are the only living things that can make their own food. Each plant is usually eaten by many different animals, and most animals eat more than one sort of living thing. To get a better idea of the feeding relationships in an area, the different food chains can be joined together to make a **food web.**

The source of all energy

Herbivores get their energy from plants. Since all plants get their energy from sunlight, the energy in herbivores originally comes from sunlight. And the energy **carnivores** get from eating other animals originally comes from sunlight, too. All living things need the Sun— without its light energy, there would be no plants or animals.

The chemical energy this lion gets by eating a zebra was originally light energy from the Sun. ⋁

photosynthesis   process by which plants use light energy to convert carbon dioxide and water into sugars and oxygen

Pyramids, pyramids

Biologists are very interested in finding out how **energy** flows through **food chains** and **food webs.** They count the number of plants and animals in a food chain and they also measure the weight of these living things. The results help biologists to understand an **ecosystem.**

Pyramids of numbers

The number of living things in a food chain can be displayed in a special bar graph. Each type of plant and animal has a different bar. A wider bar shows that there are more of that plant or animal in the food chain. The bars are stacked on top of each other to make a **pyramid of numbers.** The bar at the bottom always shows the plant at the start of the food chain.

This pyramid of numbers is for the food chain *oak tree → caterpillar → bird*. Lots of small caterpillars can feed on one large oak tree, but only a few birds can feed on all these caterpillars.

birds

caterpillars

oak tree

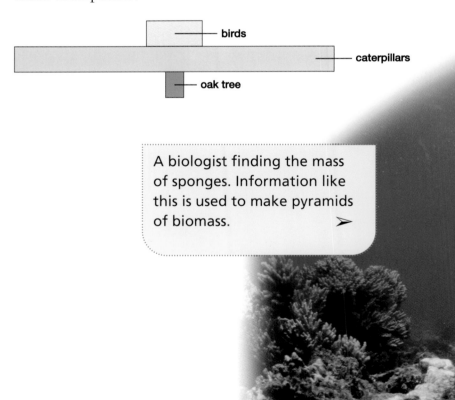

A biologist finding the mass of sponges. Information like this is used to make pyramids of biomass. ➤

biologist   scientist who studies living things
biomass   total mass of living things at each level in a food chain

Pyramids of biomass

Pyramids of biomass show the total **mass** of each type of living thing in a food chain, instead of the total number. A wide bar means a big total mass. Pyramids of biomass always get smaller as you look from bottom to top. This is because 90 percent of the energy passed on to each level is lost to the surroundings as the animals move, keep warm, and make waste. Only about 10 percent of the energy is used for growth and therefore available for eating.

The pyramid of biomass for the food chain *oak tree →
caterpillar → bird* looks very different from the pyramid of numbers. Although there is only one oak tree, it has a large mass. Birds are much heavier than caterpillars, but there are fewer of them, so their total **biomass** is smaller.

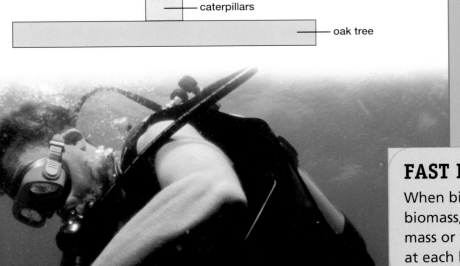

- birds
- caterpillars
- oak tree

FAST FACTS

When biologists talk about biomass, they mean the total mass or weight of living things at each level in a food chain.

ecosystem   community of animals and plants and their habitat
mass   amount of material in an object, usually measured in ounces or pounds

Burning biomass

Biomass fuel is any material from living things that can be used as a **renewable energy resource**. The most common biomass fuel is wood from trees.

Keep replanting

When wood burns, **energy** is released. The stored energy in wood originally comes from the Sun. Trees use **photosynthesis** to change light energy from the Sun into chemical energy, which is stored in the trunk and branches. When wood is burned, this chemical energy is released as heat and light energy.

Forests can be replanted with new trees after the old ones have been cut down, so wood is a renewable energy resource. More than a million homes in Australia already burn wood instead of **fossil fuels** for heating.

These willows have been coppiced. The stems are grown for firewood.

Fast-growing trees

Willow and poplar trees are often used as biomass fuel. Their stems are **coppiced** when the trees are a year old. Lots of stems grow back, and this happens so quickly that they are ready to be cut for firewood every three years.

FAST FACTS

Wood contains carbon and hydrogen. When it burns, these combine with oxygen in the air to make carbon dioxide and **water vapor**. Other substances in wood escape in the smoke or are left behind as ash.

◀ ◀ ◀ ◀ ◀ ◀ ◀ ◀

Turn back to page 20 to find out how photosynthesis works.

24   *Word store*   biomass fuel   material from living things, used as a renewable energy resource
coppiced   when the stems of trees are cut down to ground level

Using wood as a fuel

Most people have burned logs on a campfire to release heat and light energy. But burning wood in this form would not be a good way to heat homes. Smaller pieces of wood, called wood chips, are much easier to light and burn more quickly.

Steam and other gases escape when wood burns. This uses up energy and reduces the amount of heat energy given out. If wood is heated to a very high temperature while no air can get to it, these gases escape without the wood burning. A **dense**, black, solid fuel called charcoal is left behind. When a piece of charcoal is burned, it releases two times **more energy than the same mass** of wood. Charcoal is used to cook food on barbecues because it burns at a high temperature and makes very little smoke.

Electricity from wood

Wood can be burned in power stations to make electricity. The heat energy given out boils water to make steam, which then turns a **generator**. In Combined Heat and Power systems, the waste heat energy is also used to heat nearby homes.

This power station in the United States is fueled by wood chips. ⋀

dense   heavy for its size
water vapor   water in gas form

25

Some cars in Brazil run on gasohol. ∧

Biodiesel

The seeds from rape or canola crops are rich in oil and can be made into a liquid fuel called biodiesel. At the moment, it is more expensive than diesel from crude oil, but this will change as oil prices rise and more biodiesel is made. Another source of biodiesel is animal waste. The U.S. Department of Energy has invented a machine that changes 2.2 tons of chicken waste per day into fuel.

New types of biomass fuel

Material from living things can be made into liquid **biomass fuels** such as ethanol and gases such as methane. These fuels are often more useful than wood because they are a more **concentrated** source of **energy**.

Ethanol

Tiny living things called yeast can convert sugar into alcohol. This process is called **fermentation.** The alcohol formed is a clear, colorless liquid called ethanol. Ethanol burns very easily and can be used as a fuel. Because it can be made using the sugars from sugarcane plants, ethanol is a **renewable energy resource.**

In Brazil, where huge sugarcane crops grow, ethanol is mixed **with gasoline to make a fuel called gasohol. This** reduces the amount of **fossil fuels** needed to power cars there.

Rapeseed oil is used for cooking and as a fuel. ∧

concentrated   a lot crammed into a small volume
decompose   break down or decay

Biomass energy

Benefits

- Biomass fuel is a renewable energy resource, so it will never run out.
- When wood burns, it releases carbon dioxide. But biomass fuels do not increase **global warming**. Trees remove carbon dioxide from the **atmosphere** as they grow, so burning wood only puts back the carbon dioxide taken in by the growing trees.

Problems

- Wood is bulky and makes lots of smoke and ash when it burns.
- Wood is much more difficult to light than natural gas and fuels from crude oil.
- Forests are damaged if new trees are not replanted to replace those cut down.
- Ethanol and biodiesel are made from large crops, taking up land that could be used to feed people instead of fuelling vehicles.

Biogas

Animal manure is often spread on farmland because it provides nutrients for plants to grow well. As it **decomposes,** manure gives off methane gas. This "biogas" can be collected and used as a fuel for cooking or even to run small power stations. Methane can also be collected from garbage dumps, where it is given off by rotting waste.

This small biogas collector in India uses animal manure. ⱽ

fermentation   converting sugar into ethanol and carbon dioxide using yeast

global warming   extra warming of Earth cause by an increased greenhouse effect

Wind Energy

The wind has a lot of kinetic energy in it. Very strong winds can rip up trees and damage buildings.

If you have ever flown a kite on a windy day, you will know how powerful the wind can be. The **kinetic energy** in wind can be used to drive all sorts of machinery. It can even be turned into electrical **energy**.

Where does the wind come from?

When air warms up, it **expands** and rises upward. When air cools, it **contracts** and sinks downward. When the Sun is shining, some parts of Earth's surface become warmer than others. Where the surface is warm, the air above it rises. Air from cooler places rushes in to replace the warm air. This movement of air causes winds. Big differences in temperature can cause very strong winds.

Measuring the wind

The Beaufort scale is used to **estimate** the power of wind. Litter blows around at force 4 and twigs break off trees at force 8. A force 12 wind is **hurricane** force, with wind speeds of more than 74 miles (120 kilometers) per hour.

Sailing ships have sailed across the oceans of the world for thousands of years using the kinetic energy of wind to move them.

FAST FACTS

On the coast, the wind blows in from the sea during the day and out to sea at night.

Word store   contract   become smaller and fill less space
expand   get bigger

A renewable energy resource

Because heat energy from the Sun is turned into kinetic energy in the wind, wind is a **renewable energy resource**. As long as the Sun's heat energy continues to warm Earth, we will be able to get energy from the wind.

Sailing

Sailing ships use large sails to harness the wind's kinetic energy. Very large sailing ships have several **masts** with many sails on them. It takes a lot of kinetic energy from the wind to get them moving. Modern sailing ships usually have a diesel-powered engine, in case the wind dies down.

Windsurfing

Windsurfers use kinetic energy from the wind to speed along the surface of the sea. The force of the wind pushing on the sail tries to tip the board on its side, so the surfer has to lean back to stay balanced.

Windsurfers use kinetic energy from the wind.

hurricane   very powerful storm
mast   upright pole that supports the sails on a boat

Moving machinery

Sailing ships move forward using the **kinetic energy** in the wind. But windmills use the kinetic energy in the wind in a different way—to turn machinery.

Windmills

Windmills have sails to catch the wind, just like a sailing ship. But the sails on a windmill spin around in circles. They are split into two or more **blades** that are twisted or tilted slightly. If they were just flat, they would not spin.

Steel wind pumps, often seen in cowboy movies, pump water to irrigate crops. ⋀

From wind to water

In parts of the world where it does not often rain, crops can be **irrigated** with water pumped from underground. Steel wind pumps were first made over a hundred years ago. They are cheap and reliable, so they are still used on many farms.

30   *Word store*   blade   spinning arm on a windmill or turbine
irrigate   to water crops when there is not enough rain

Windmills work best when they face the wind. With the first windmills, someone had to turn the blades to face the wind. In 1745 Edmund Lee invented the fantail. The wind pushes small sails on the fantail so that the windmill turns to face the wind on its own.

Early days

The name *windmill* comes from the first type of work people did using **energy** from the wind. Wheat must be ground into flour before it can be used to make bread. This is called milling. Windmills were often used in the past to turn the milling machinery, which ground the wheat between two heavy stone wheels. Since then, windmills have been used for many different tasks.

Land from the sea

Extra land for farms and buildings has been **reclaimed** from the sea in many parts of the world. The Netherlands has a lot of land that was once under the sea. Barriers were built behind the seashore and the seawater was pumped away into canals, leaving dry land behind. Windmills connected to water pumps were used to do this job. Once built, they could keep pumping water away with very low **running costs.**

Savonius turbines can be made cheaply from old oil drums. They are used to drive farm machinery.

Traditional windmills, like this one in England, were used for pumping water to drain land or for grinding cereal grain to make flour.

Finnish windmills

Savonius wind **turbines** were invented in Finland in the 1920s by Sigrid Savonius. They look very different from other windmills. Seen from the top, their blades have an S-shape so that they always face the wind.

reclaim   to make land useful again
turbine   machinery that is turned by moving air, water, or steam

Electricity from the wind

Most modern windmills are wind **turbines.** They turn **generators** to make electricity. The electricity is transferred to offices and homes where it can easily be changed into other types of **energy,** such as heat or light.

Designed to go faster

The old windmills were good at turning heavy machinery at low speeds, but to make electricity, modern windmills have to spin very quickly. They use two or three thin **blades** that look like airplane propellers. These blades can be up to 130 feet (40 meters) long. They are fixed on top of tall towers so that they do not scrape the ground. The blades are joined by a series of **gears** to a generator in the top of the tower. As long as the wind is blowing, the generator will **turn and make electricity.**

Wind farms can be quite noisy, so they are often built away from people. ⋀

Farming the wind

Lots of windmills are often built together in a windy place to make a **wind farm.** Because the blades are on tall towers, the land underneath them can still be used for growing crops and grazing animals.

Some modern designs for windmills look very different from the traditional ones. This design does not need a tall tower. ➢

FAST FACTS

Traditional windmills changed about a sixth of the energy in the wind passing through their blades into useful energy for turning machinery. Modern windmills are much more efficient, converting almost half of the energy in the wind into useful energy for generating electricity.

gear   equipment that can change the speed of turning machinery

Wind power

Benefits

- Windmills of all designs do not need any fuel to run them.
- They do not make any **pollution**.
- Once the wind turbines have been built, their **running costs** are low.
- Turbines last up to 25 years before they get worn out and need replacing.

Problems

- Windmills only work on windy days.
- They must be shut down if the wind is blowing too hard.
- Only some parts of a country are windy enough for wind farms, and these are often on top of hills.
- Some people do not like wind farms because they can spoil views of the countryside.
- **Offshore** wind farms may not spoil the view, but they are more expensive to build than those on land.

Danish windmills

Wind turbines are used all over the world, and Denmark makes about half of them. A fifth of Denmark's electricity is made by wind power. One offshore wind farm has 80 turbines.

This is an offshore wind turbine. The base sits on the seabed. ◄

offshore built out at sea
wind farm lots of wind turbines in one place

33

Energy from Moving Water

Moving water can be extremely powerful. Just like the **kinetic energy** in wind, the kinetic energy in moving water can be used to drive all sorts of machinery, including electricity **generators.**

The water cycle

Water **evaporates** from the surfaces of seas and lakes to form **water vapor**, which rises into the sky. The water vapor cools and **condenses** to make clouds of tiny water droplets. These droplets clump together and fall to the ground as rain. Most rain happens over the sea, but when it falls onto the land, it flows into rivers. **Gravity makes these rivers flow back to the sea or into lakes. This is called the water cycle.**

A river flows quickly down a steep mountainside. ∧

Rivers and seas

About 97 percent of Earth's water is sea water. Most of the rest is frozen as ice in icebergs, **glaciers**, and the **polar ice caps.** Rivers contain just one millionth of Earth's water, but nearly all our drinking water comes from them.

condensation

evaporation

rain, snow, or hail

heated by the Sun

water runs off land into oceans

This is the water cycle. Heat energy from the Sun keeps the cycle going. ➢

Word store   condense   to change from gas to liquid
evaporate   to change from liquid to gas

A renewable energy resource

Heat **energy** from the Sun drives the water cycle because it evaporates water from the surfaces of seas and lakes. As long as the Sun heats water on Earth's surface, the water cycle will keep on going. This means that the kinetic energy in flowing rivers is a **renewable energy resource.**

Water mills

Water mills are built next to rivers. They use kinetic energy in the moving water to turn machinery. A large steel or wooden waterwheel is built on to the side of the mill. Waterwheels have flat **blades** all around them so that the moving water turns them. They turn slowly, but they are very powerful. They can drive machinery for grinding wheat, pumping water, or weaving cloth.

Stored energy

If there is no rain for a long time, rivers may flow too slowly to turn a waterwheel. To get around this problem, water is stored in millponds. If the river begins to dry out, the stored water is let out of the pond to turn the waterwheel.

FAST FACTS
Before steam power, many towns were built near rivers so waterwheels could be used.

A waterwheel turns on the side of a water mill.

glacier   very large sheet of ice found in cold parts of the world
gravity   force that makes objects fall downward

Hydroelectric power

Gravity makes water flow from high places to low places. The moving water contains **kinetic energy**. **Hydroelectric power** stations are able to change the kinetic energy in moving water into electrical **energy**.

Electricity from moving water

In a hydroelectric power station, part of a river's flow is sent through pipes. The water turns **turbines** in the pipes, and the turbines turn electricity **generators**. The water is returned to the river further downstream. This works well if the river is large with lots of water flowing in it.

The further water falls, the faster it flows and the more kinetic energy it contains. If water is made to fall from a great height, a lot of electricity can be made. **Dams** are often used to store water and increase the height from which the water falls. This is a large-scale version of the millpond idea for waterwheels.

The Dinorwig power station uses more energy than it produces to pump water back up the mountain. But this is the only way it can produce enough energy at **peak periods.** ∧

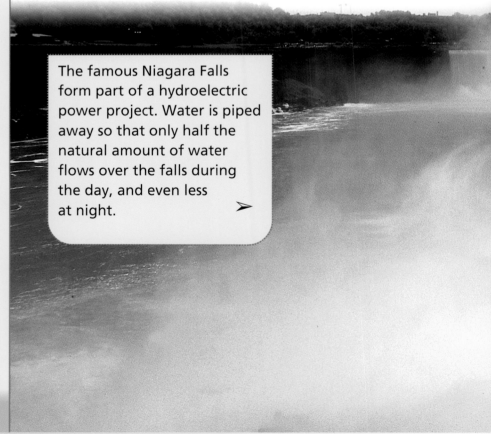

The famous Niagara Falls form part of a hydroelectric power project. Water is piped away so that only half the natural amount of water flows over the falls during the day, and even less at night. ➤

Electric mountain

Electricity is cheaper at night because fewer people want to use it. The Dinorwig hydroelectric power station in Wales makes electricity during the day, when lots of people need it. At night, cheap electricity is used to pump water back up to the reservoir ready for the next day. The cheap electricity cannot just be kept for the next day because it is difficult to store.

Word store   dam   barrier built across a river to block it so that water can be stored
hydroelectric power   electricity made using the energy in moving water

Dam building

It is best to build a dam in a hilly area with steep valley sides. In this way, a lot of water is stored high up without flooding too much land. Gates control the flow of water from the **reservoir** behind the dam into the turbines. Hydroelectric power stations can be started in seconds simply by opening the gates.

FAST FACTS

The biggest water storage project in the world is the Three Gorges in China. If the concrete in its dams were divided up, there would be enough concrete to give everyone in the world a 22-pound (10-kilogram) block!

The Hoover Dam

The Hoover Dam was built on the Colorado River between 1931 and 1936. Its turbines can make all the electricity needed by a city of 750,000 people. During peak periods, enough water runs through the turbines to fill 15 swimming pools every second.

This is the Hoover Dam. The reservoir behind the dam is called Lake Mead. It has an area of 229 square miles (593 square kilometers).

peak period   time when most electricity is needed
reservoir   large lake behind a dam, used for storing water

Tidal power

Most **hydroelectric power** stations use the **energy** in moving river water to make electricity. The energy needed to get the water into the rivers comes from the Sun, as part of the water cycle. The energy needed to move the water downhill comes from Earth's **gravity.** Tidal power uses seawater that moves for a very different reason—the Moon's gravity.

Moon power

The Moon's gravity pulls the water in Earth's seas toward it. This makes the sea level bulge wherever Earth is facing the Moon—it is high tide there. The sea level goes down elsewhere, making it low tide. As Earth spins, different places face the Moon, so they get high and low tides at **different times during the day and night.**

Regular orbit

The Moon is Earth's natural **satellite.** It travels all the way around Earth once every 28 days. The Moon's gravity causes the oceans to bulge as it moves around Earth. On ground level, we see this effect in the tides.

The world's biggest tidal barrage is at La Rance, France. Built in 1966, it is 820 yards (750 meters) long. It makes as much electricity as a small coal power station— enough for 20,000 homes. ➤

barrage   long dam built across a bay or river

Tidal barrages

To use the **kinetic energy** of tidal water, a long **dam** called a **barrage** is built across a bay or river. It is only worth building if the water level changes by 16 to 33 feet (5 to 10 meters) between tides, and if there is a large area behind the barrage to store water at high tide. Tubes inside the barrage let seawater in and out as the tide changes. The moving water turns **turbines** inside the tubes, and the turbines turn electricity **generators**.

Some tidal barrages only make electricity as the tide goes out. Seawater is stored behind them as the tide comes in, then released through the turbines after the tide has gone out again. Others, like the barrage at La Rance in France, make electricity as the tide comes in as well.

Wave

A river flows out to sea at its mouth. But in some rivers, such as the Severn in England and the Río Araguari in Brazil, a strange thing can happen when the tide comes in. The sea pushes the river water back upstream, making a powerful wave called a bore.

Tidal bores can travel several miles inland. It is even possible to surf on them!

Floaters

Floaters are wave machines that bob up and down on the surface of the sea. As they do this, they change the up-and-down movement of the water into a turning movement that drives an electricity **generator**. One design, called the Salter's Duck, can change 90 percent of the energy in a wave into electricity.

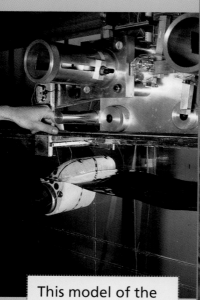

This model of the Salter's Duck is being tested in a laboratory. ⋀

Wave power

Your hands get hot if you rub them together quickly. This is because of **friction**—the force that tries to stop one object from moving over another. The friction changes some of the **kinetic energy** from your moving hands into heat **energy**. Friction between the wind and the surface of the sea makes waves. It causes kinetic energy to transfer from the moving air to the water. The kinetic energy in waves can be used to make electricity.

Up and down

When ocean waves reach shallow water at a beach, they curl over and break. But if you stand in deeper water, you will see that the water just rises and falls as the waves go past. Wave-power machines use this up-and-down movement to **make electricity. Scientists are still experimenting to find the best design for trapping energy from waves.**

Surfers use the kinetic energy in waves to push them into shore at great speeds. ⋀

friction   force that tries to stop one object from moving over another

Water power

Benefits

- Waterwheels, **hydroelectric power stations**, tidal **barrages** and wave machines do not need any fuel to run them.
- They do not make any **pollution**
- **Running costs** are low.
- They are very reliable.
- **Dams** and tidal barrages can be also used as bridges across rivers and bays.

Problems

- Dams flood a lot of land, affecting local wildlife and destroying homes.
- The building costs are usually very high.
- Many of the places suitable for building are far from cities, so a lot of cable is needed to supply the electricity.
- Flooded trees make methane as they rot away, which increases **global warming**.
- Mud builds up behind dams, making them less useful.
- Fields downstream of a dam get fewer **minerals** for growing crops.

Sitters

Sitters are wave machines that are fixed in one place. As the waves move, they squeeze air inside the machines. The squeezed air turns a **turbine,** which then turns an electricity generator. The Limpet, built on the Scottish island of Islay, makes enough electricity for 300 houses.

Waves crashing onto the Limpet wave machine.

FAST FACTS

The total energy in the oceans' waves is enough to make twice the electricity needed by the whole world. But we can only trap a tiny percentage of this energy at the moment.

What Next?

Share it out

Peak periods for electricity use are different for different countries. For example, France has slightly different peak times than Great Britain. An underwater electricity cable links the two countries, so that one country's cheaper **off-peak** electricity can be used by the other country during peak times.

Fossil fuels will run out one day, even if we all try to save **energy.** But as long as light and heat energy from the Sun reach Earth, **renewable energy resources** will never run out. At some point in the future, all the world's energy and electricity needs will have to come from renewable resources. What will this future world be like?

Big is beautiful?

Most of the equipment and machines described in this book are big. Some of them, such as wind **turbines, dams,** and tidal **barrages,** are very big. Building them may change the landscape a lot. The Three Gorges **hydroelectric power** project in China moved a million people and over a thousand factories to make way for the new **reservoir.** Will the future **bring us more of these big projects, or something else?**

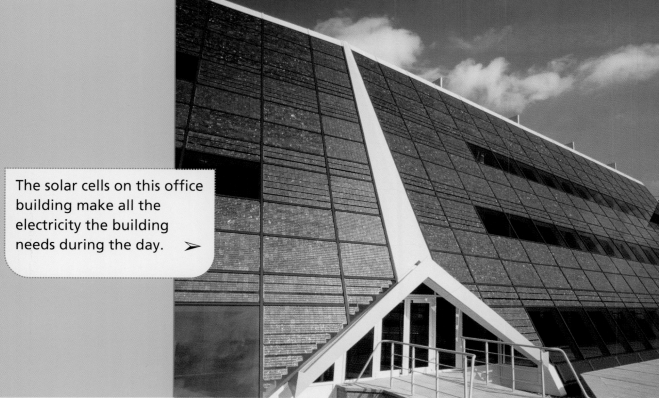

The solar cells on this office building make all the electricity the building needs during the day. ➤

navigation buoy   marker in the sea for shipping
off-peak   time when less electricity is needed

Small is better?

Architects can design buildings to use renewable energy resources on a smaller scale. **Solar** panels can be easily added to roofs to heat water. Small wind turbines and solar cells built into the walls and roofs can make electricity for the building. Any extra electricity can be sold to the main electricity grid to supply other users.

On an even smaller scale, there are many pieces of equipment that can be powered by renewable energy resources. These include calculators, traffic lights, and **navigation buoys** out at sea. Expect to see an exciting mix of all sorts of renewable energy resources being used everywhere in the future.

FAST FACTS
Insulating a house can reduce the amount of energy it uses by up to 90 percent.

Micro power
Hydroelectric power stations do not have to be big. Small ones, called micro-hydroelectric stations, make electricity for villages without a main electricity supply. Some of a nearby river's flow is sent through a pipe to turn a turbine and **generator**. The water is returned to the river downstream, so the environment is not damaged.

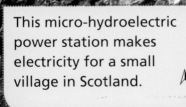

This micro-hydroelectric power station makes electricity for a small village in Scotland. ⋀

Find Out More

Organizations

Understanding Energy

Information and quizzes about renewable energy resources and generating electricity.
energy.org.uk

Wind Energy

Information and a film about the Danish wind energy industry. The website includes instructions on making your own model wind **turbine**.
windpower.org

Dr. E's Energy Lab

Lots of information about renewable energy resources and links to other websites.
eere.energy.gov/kids

Renewable Energy

Includes ideas for using renewable energy in the home and up-to-date news.
greenhouse.gov.au/renewable

Books

Oxlade, Chris. *Science Topics: Energy*. Chicago: Heinemann Library, 2000.

Parker, Steve. *Energy Files: Water, Solar, Wind*. Chicago: Heinemann Library, 2002.

Saunders, Nigel, and Steven Chapman. *Energy Essentials: Fossil Fuel*. Chicago: Raintree, 2004.

Sneddon, Robert. *Energy for Life: Energy Alternatives*. Chicago: Heinemann Library, 2002.

World Wide Web

If you want to find out more about **renewable energy,** you can search the Internet using keywords such as these:

- "renewable energy"
- "alternative energy"
- biodiesel + **biomass**
- **"hydroelectric power"**
- "tidal power"
- "wave power"
- "wind energy"

You can also make your own keywords by using headings or words from this book. Use the search tips opposite to help you find the most useful websites.

Search tips

There are billions of pages on the Internet, so it can be difficult to find exactly what you want to find. For example, if you just type in "energy" on a search engine such as Google, you will get a list of 35 million web pages. These search skills will help you find useful websites more quickly:

- Use simple keywords instead of whole sentences.

- Use two to six keywords in a search, putting the most important words first.

- Be precise—only use names of people, places, or things.

- If you want to find words that go together, put quotation marks around them—for example "tidal power" or "wind energy."

- Use the advanced section of your search engine.

- Use the "+" sign between keywords to link them.

Where to search

Search engine

A search engine looks through the entire web and lists all sites that match the words in the search box. It can give thousands of links, but the best matches are at the top of the list, on the first page. Try **www.google.com.**

Search directory

A search directory is like a library of websites that have been sorted by a person instead of a computer. You can search by keyword or subject and browse through the different sites like you look through books on a library shelf. A good example is **yahooligans.com.**

Glossary

absorb to take in

architect designer of buildings

Arctic far north, where it is usually very cold

atmosphere layer of gases that surround a planet like Earth

barrage long dam built across a bay or river

barrel unit used to measure the volume of crude oil; one barrel is 42 gal (159 l)

billion one thousand million

biologist scientist who studies living things

biomass total mass of living things at each level in a food chain

biomass fuel material from living things, used as a renewable energy resource

blade spinning arm on a windmill or turbine

carnivore animal that eats other animals

cell tiny building block of living things

chemical reaction change in which new substances are made and energy is given out or taken in

chlorophyll green substance that absorbs light energy, found in plants

concentrated a lot crammed into a small volume

condense to change from gas to liquid

contract become smaller and fill less space

coppiced when the stems of trees are cut down to ground level

dam barrier built across a river to block it so that water can be stored

decompose to break down or decay

dense heavy for its size

dilute mixed with another substance, usually water

dull not shiny

ecosystem community of animals and plants and their habitat

electron tiny, negatively charged particle outside the nucleus of an atom

energy ability to do work; light, heat, and electricity are types of energy

energy resource source or store of energy, such as hydroelectric power and coal

estimate to judge or work out roughly

evaporate to change from liquid to gas

expand get bigger

fermentation converting sugar into ethanol and carbon dioxide using yeast

focus to concentrate into one spot

food chain list of living things ordered by what eats what

food web two or more food chains joined together

fossil fuel fuel formed from the remains of ancient plants and animals

friction force that tries to stop one object from moving over another

gear equipment that can change the speed of turning machinery

generator equipment used to make electricity

glacier very large sheet of ice found in cold parts of the world

global warming extra warming of Earth caused by an increased greenhouse effect

gravity force that makes objects fall downward

greenhouse effect keeping the atmosphere warm by trapping heat

herbivore animal that eats plants

hurricane very powerful storm

hydroelectric power electricity made using the energy in moving water

insulated covered in material that reduces heat loss

irrigate to water crops when there is not enough rain

kinetic energy energy of moving things

mass amount of material in an object, usually measured in ounces or pounds

mast upright pole that supports the sails on a boat

megawatt one million watts—one million joules of energy released every second

mineral substance needed by plants and animals to keep them healthy

navigation buoy marker in the sea for shipping

nonrenewable resource that will run out one day and cannot be replaced

off-peak time when less electricity is needed

offshore built out at sea

parabola U-shaped curve

passive something that happens with no machinery or extra energy needed

peak period time when most electricity is needed

pests insects and fungi that damage plants

photosynthesis process by which plants use light energy to convert carbon dioxide and water into sugars and oxygen

photovoltaic effect converting light energy into electrical energy

piston moving cylinder in an engine or other piece of machinery

polar ice caps ice covering the North and South poles of Earth

pollute to add harmful substances to the air, water, or land

pollution harmful substances in the air, water, or on land

pyramid of biomass graph showing the mass of each type of living thing in a food chain

pyramid of numbers graph showing the total number of each type of living thing in a food chain

rationed given a fixed amount of something

reclaim make land useful again

refined purified at an oil refinery

renewable will not run out and can be replaced

reservoir large lake behind a dam, used for storing water

running cost cost of keeping equipment working

satellite object that orbits a planet

solar anything to do with the Sun

transparent see through

turbine machinery that is turned by moving air, water, or steam

water vapor water in gas form

wind farm lots of wind turbines in one place

Index